MIMIKA COONEY

Write the Right Book

Marketing Strategies for Writers

mimika

This book was professionally typeset on Reedsy.
Find out more at reedsy.com

Contents

IV   Part Four

Invitation

As a thank you for purchasing this book, I would love to gift you with the print-able **Book Writing Checklist**. Print out this tool to help you work through the book as you follow along. Download here www.mimikacooney.com/rightbook

WRITE THE RIGHT BOOK

FREE CHECKLIST
WWW.MIMIKACOONEY.COM/RIGHTBOOK

I

Part One

1

Busting Myths

A s writers, we have a vision for what we want to say, but sometimes there are beliefs that hold us back. These false beliefs can cause us to get disappointed, or worse, cause us to give up on our quest to write a book. Perhaps you've believed these, too?

When I sit down to write, it will just come.

Writers are born, not made.

I'm terrible at English, so I can't right a book.

There are already books on the subject that I want to write about, so why add another one?

Writing a book is hard.

My book idea is totally unique because no one else has written about it.

A book has to have a large word count for it to sell.

A book can only be traditionally published.

If you're not a natural writer, it takes discipline to get yourself into a flow. But once you have a system, there are means and ways and tools available today that you can use to get your book written and published very fast.

Perhaps you've heard that a book has to be very long in order for it to sell. This is not necessarily true in today's society as people don't have a lot of time and prefer to consume content faster. The quicker you can get them information (and they can consume it), the better.

If your book is totally unique and no one is writing about it, that is a big red flag that there is not a market for it.

This book is going to share strategies on how you can break through these myths and barriers, so you can get your book out into the world. The world needs what you have to say, and they need it now!

2

Why Write a Book?

There are many reasons and motivations to write a book. Perhaps your motivation is to become a full-time author? Maybe your goal is to make money by selling your coaching or consulting services? Maybe you want to be invited to speak on stage? Perhaps you're a subject matter expert, and you want to teach what you know in courses and workshops? Perhaps you want to start a movement, or you want to start and grow a ministry or a church?

In a Christian writers Facebook group, the question was asked, "What is your reason for wanting to write a book?" and some of the answers included:

"Because I have a unique perspective and experience with my topic."

"To help others down this jagged road I have been on. To heal by helping."

"To help others by offering them perspective, hope, and encouragement from a lens that I have been given through my life experience and in practice of serving others."

"Because I love to write and love to read books."

"To help others in their struggles know they're not alone; to point them to that ever-brightening hope."

"I want to write a book because there is life and light inside of me."

"To encourage women in marriages that seem hopeless."

"To motivate people to let their light shine!"

"To leave something for the future family members and to share my life."

"To offer inspiration, beauty, encouragement, happiness, delight, and laughter in the mundane of the daily."

"Because it bugs me until I write it down!"

"To leave people's hearts a bit lighter after they lay the book down."

"Because I have a book in me that can't not come out."

"I believe my story is meant to encourage others."

"I can't not write. Even if I don't get it down on paper, my mind is continually writing."

"To help others with trauma and grief. To tell my own story after losing my 9-year-old in a car accident."

Writing a book is great for any one of these reasons. A book will be the best tool to open doors, share your story, connect with people, generate leads, and establish you as an authority in your niche.

I firmly believe that a book is the best business card you can have. Whether you are in business or in ministry, or you have an inspiring message to share, putting your knowledge and expertise into a book format is one of the easiest ways of sharing information.

Reasons Why You Should Publish a Book

1. To weave a Personal Testimony or Story of Hope to help and motivate others.

Once you have experienced a life-changing event, you either come out bitter or better. No one wants to read about someone who is still bleeding on the page from their past hurts. It's imperative you work through the process before putting pen to paper. When you've moved through the process of healing and acceptance, then you are ready to share your story.

2. To record some of your Life's Major Events and for Posterity.

Think of your book as a recording of your experiences for future generations to appreciate. If this is your primary goal, then it's considered a vanity project and doesn't require you follow the publishing rules. You could pursue the path of self-publishing direct to Amazon or digital for the most cost-effective method. This would allow you to set up a print-on-demand option, where you don't have to spend on printing thousands of copies. Instead of having books gathering dust in your garage, you will print as you need them. Some of my favorite resources for this are [1]Draft2Digital; [2]BookBaby; [3]Lulu Press; [4] Ingram Spark; and of course, [5]Amazon KDP.

3. To make some additional Money.

I'll be honest, nobody gets rich on book sales alone, unless you are a celebrity. You need a long-term plan and a robust marketing strategy. You can make a living if you put in the work. Ideally, you want to create a library of at least 20 books and build that over 2 to 5 years. Where the big money lies is thinking of your book as a tool. This will lead to either consulting, coaching, courses, or speaking opportunities (i.e. backend sales).

4. To become a Full-time Writer.

If you have a goal to become a full-time author, then you do need a 5- to 10-year plan and strategy to get you there. You need around 20 books in your collection for the passive income stream to be at a sustainable level. You also need to be serious about building your author platform. Focus on getting

---

[1] Draft2Digital http://bit.ly/2s6tJQ2

[2] Book Baby https://www.bookbaby.com

[3] Lulu Press https://www.lulu.com

[4] Ingram Spark https://ingramspark.com

[5] Amazon KDP https://kdp.amazon.com

your name known and leverage the relationships you have. If you know of celebrities or other big names who can help promote you, it will help to boost your visibility. You will also need to invest in paying for ads through either Amazon or Facebook to continue to grow your audience and drive book sales.

5. To become a Professional Speaker.

Using your book as a tool or business card is a great way of opening doors to speaking. Speaking gigs vary in pay. If you welcome an invitation to speak at a church, many churches don't pay at all. However, they do allow back of room sales where you can set up a table and sign books. This works well once you've built up a network and a following so people are excited to hear you speak.

6. To Establish Authority and/or Grow a Business.

As a subject matter expert, you can collate your knowledge into a book. This works as a lead generation tool for your business. They say having a book is the best business card you can have! It elevates your brand authority in a market and creates opportunities. This leads prospects down a funnel toward purchasing your products or more higher-end programs. Self-publishing your own book will ensure you keep control and reap the profits.

The Reality of Publishing

1. Your story does matter, but nobody cares unless it's about the reader. Identifying your target market is key for all future decisions. Write for the market, versus trying to find a market for your writing. Knowing what market you are writing for is the first piece of the puzzle.

2. The truth is that memoirs or autobiographies don't sell well (unless you are a celebrity or are well-known). Many non-fiction writers make this mistake of thinking that they have to tell their whole life story in a chronological manner. Unfortunately, it does not read or sell well. The solution is to think of the life lessons you're trying to share. For example,

if you write it more for the Christian Living space as a non-fiction teaching book, you will find a better fit. Focusing on a micro moment or major life lesson works better.

3. Successful book sales is all about positioning and how the book is placed amongst others that are similar. Think of "how to overcome/discover/unlock-/learn" etc. My own book [6]*Worrier to Warrior: A Mother's Journey from Fear to Faith* started as a memoir but I altered it to fit within the Women's Christian Living category.

4. Self-publishing a book requires an investment of money even if you do it yourself. The key is to do it professionally if you want your investment to pay dividends. You don't want to skimp on a cheap cover or eliminate editing. Conservatively, you could get a professionally designed cover done for $30 to $100. You also need to invest in hiring a professional editor/proofreader before publishing.

5. Authors make the mistake of thinking that by simply pressing publish, that a book will sell itself. The reality is books don't sell themselves. The author is in charge of all the marketing and promotion. This is true even if you get a publishing contract with a big name publisher. They still expect you to do most of the legwork of book promotion. This is why building an online presence (website, social media, email list) is vital for continued success.

6. Nobody cares about your experience unless you make it about how it helps the reader solve their problem or find a solution. This is especially true when writing for the non-fiction market. If you want to write it simply as a story, then consider it more of a work of entertainment and focus on the fiction market.

So now you have some food for thought. You've got decisions to make about the route you want to take. Once you pick the path, then the steps will become easier.

---

[6] Worrier to Warrior: A Mother's Journey from Fear to Faith https://www.mimikacooney.com/warriorlinks

Next Steps:

- Decide how you want to position your book before you go to the effort of writing the wrong book.
- Do the research and find the correct category and keywords.
- Finish writing your story and first draft.
- Find a professional editor/proofreader and have them tidy the manuscript to make it print-ready.
- Hire a good graphic designer to create the book cover, or buy a ready-made one on the [7]Book Cover Designers; [8]Creative Market; or [9]Self Pub Book Covers.
- Get to work building your [10]Author Platform and brand. You need to have your audience primed and ready for when your book launches.

---

[7] Book Cover Designers https://thebookcoverdesigner.com/

[8] Creative Market http://bit.ly/2N1IPxe

[9] Self Pub Book Covers https://selfpubbookcovers.com/

[10] Build Your Author Platform with a Purpose: Marketing Strategies for Writers (Book 2) https://www.mimikacooney.com/platformlinks

3

Common Mistakes Writers Make

The idea of writing a book can seem so glamorous. We romance the idea of what it would be like to be a published author. Then the overwhelm sets in and the hard work really begins. Here are some common mistakes that aspiring writers make and how to avoid them.

Mistake #1 - Not Having a Plan or Strategy

Throwing a book out there and just hoping that Amazon will sell it for you is called hope marketing. It simply doesn't work like that. It's very important to have a strategy. I don't know about you, but I love lists. I have to have a list that I can tick off so I feel like I've actually achieved something. It gives me a way of staying focused. I can suffer from distraction very easily and go down these little rabbit holes with every little shiny thing that comes along. This is why it's important to have a branding strategy or blueprint, an understanding of who I am and whom I serve. When you have opportunities come across your path, you can easily say no or yes because you know if it fits within your blueprint and plan.

Start with the end in mind. Where do you want to end up with your goal? Is it to become a paid speaker, launch a product or program, or become a full-time author? Writing a book is an awesome way to start because it is the best business card. If you want to write a series of books, think about the series and work your way back.

Keeping up with social media can be a total time suck. That is why strategy and planning are so important. Knowing what you want to achieve is crucial as every platform functions differently. The way you treat Instagram is different from the way you use Facebook, but again, it first depends on discovering where your ideal audience is.

Mistake #2 - Writing the Wrong Book

Writing the wrong book will cost you time, money, and loads of frustration. Many writers get disappointed when their book doesn't sell well because it doesn't resonate with an audience. For instance, I had this whole plan for writing a memoir and plan for the chronological order of what I wanted to say, but I realized it was the wrong book! Even though it was painful to hear, it saved me six months of hard work writing a book that no one would want to read. That is why it's so important to do ample research for the categories, audience, keywords, and positioning *before* writing a single word. This is exactly what a publisher would do to find the perfect market fit for a book idea.

Mistake #3 - Writing for Yourself and Not the Audience

Many creators and artists make the mistake of writing a book or creating a product for themselves and not an audience. When you are starting out, you want to share your story with the world. You want to write from your perspective because you feel justified by what you've experienced. However, if it's not for the right audience or how *they* see things, your writing is going to fall on deaf ears. Consider who that person is. Who is sitting on the other end of the table? Who is the reader, or the listener, or the audience? Where is she in her life and what is she doing? What is she thinking about, and how can you help her?

Mistake #4 - Ignoring the Need to Build a Platform

In marketing and publishing, we talk about platform. It's when someone has a voice, has something to say, and uses methods to share their message with a wider audience. Whether it's speaking on stage, making videos, writing books, or creating products, you need a platform if you want your message to spread far and wide. A platform is built mostly online these days through TV, YouTube, radio, websites, blogs, magazines, or social media.

A platform helps you to be seen and heard above the crowd. If you want to be someone of influence that others notice, you need to get over yourself. You need a platform. It's not about putting your art out there hoping that if you build it, they will come. Sorry to disappoint you, but that simply doesn't work anymore. Times have changed and technology has changed the competitive landscape. If you're serious about your message, then you need to take building your platform seriously as one of your main priorities. Think of it this way: you have something valuable to teach but you're teaching to an empty classroom. We need to get those bums on seats!

Mistake #5 - Not Treating a Platform Like a Business

Not treating platform-building like a business is like throwing spaghetti against the wall hoping it will stick. Trying random tactics or marketing methods based on what everyone else is doing is often not very effective, and utterly exhausting. You need to think about your efforts just like someone running a business. Where is your audience and what daily tasks can I do to put myself in front of them? When you think of it as a business, you will be consistent with your efforts and measure your results.

Mistake #6 - Copying Other People's Ideas and Getting Frustrated When It Doesn't Work

Using someone else's process can be a waste of time, especially when the important middle steps are skipped. What you see online can be deceiving. You might hear someone say, "Just do this and you'll get this immediate result and make millions of dollars!" That is just not true. It may look like plain sailing, but underneath they are flapping furiously like a duck on water in a storm. There are a lot of important steps that you might be missing out on. You don't have to do it the same way as everyone else, but you can shortcut your efforts when you make decisions based on what will work for you.

Mistake #7 - Ignoring the Importance of a Professionally Designed Cover

People do judge a book by its cover. It's a simple fact. How are they going to read what you have written if the cover is not enticing? Think about how they promote movies. You will notice that the covers and movie posters that sell well are clean, bright, and the messaging is clear and precise. Often, professional photography is used with either the author, actors, or models to tell a story with crisp quality. I see this so many times with newbie authors and it hurts my eyeballs. When you go cheap designing a cover by doing it yourself (when you're not a designer), it looks cheap and negatively affects the perceived value of the content. Or they pick a cover with a photo or artwork because it's sentimental or meaningful to them personally, but has no connection on what the book is about. Most writers are not designers and have no clue what good design looks like. I like to think of my book cover just like a movie poster with all the right cues and feels.

Admittedly, I personally have designed some of my own book covers and taken the photos myself. This is only because I've been a professional photographer and graphic designer for 15 years. However, I still get feedback from other designers and my audience to make sure my book covers are resonating and telling the right story. I do a ton of research within the category to assess if my design idea aligns with the content. I have the personal belief that if I'm going to do something, I'm going to do it well. Why would I cheapen the importance of my work by slapping together poorly designed packaging? It's important to put in the effort to ensure you are making a good first impression.

No matter whether you are self-publishing or working through a publisher, the cover needs to look professional. If you are not a graphic designer, make sure to hire someone who is. You can find very talented designers and professional photographers at affordable prices on places like [11]Reedsy; [12] Fiverr; [13]99designs; or [14]Upwork. You can also buy ready-made covers online through [15]Creative Market or [16]Etsy.

Mistake #8 - Not Hiring a Professional Editor and Proofreader

When starting out, it can be tempting to omit paying for an editor or proof-reader, especially when you're on a tight budget. However, bad grammar and typos will soon be apparent in the bad reviews you receive. With the first run of my book, I had read it, re-read it, and had 10 friends and family proofread it. I was horrified to discover that there were still errors after it went to print! The good thing about self-publishing is that I could quickly correct the mistakes without having to fork out on a huge print run. Hiring an editor may seem expensive, but it will save you time and be one of the best investments you can make.

---

[11] Reedsy http://bit.ly/2T2kjzW

[12] Fiverr http://bit.ly/2T0gFGN

[13] 99 Designs http://bit.ly/37LKFu2

[14] Upwork https://www.upwork.com

[15] Creative Market http://bit.ly/2N1IPxe

[16] Etsy https://www.etsy.com/

Mistake #9 - Expecting that the Publisher Will Do All the Marketing

The traditional publishing industry is a business and their goal is to make money from publishing books. They have a very narrow focus of who they like to publish based on past performance. They have limited resources and they will prefer to hedge their bets on an author with a proven track record. Unless you're a big name, publishers don't want to do the hard work of promotion unless they have a guarantee of success. They'll add fuel to the fire, but they expect you to start the spark. Many bestselling authors you see that are backed by a big publisher have a large following and they are guaranteed to sell their books. You can have a stake in the ground by showing publishers that you've got what it takes by building your assets and platform right now. This will help you better position yourself to have your book acquisitioned in the future.

Mistake #10 - Giving Up before Starting

No one becomes an overnight success; that's not real life. Think about how many authors, singers, restaurants, and entrepreneurs are in the world. Just because there is competition doesn't mean you should give up or not even try. Competition is fierce, but don't let that deter you. Everybody has an idea, and everyone thinks their idea is original. In an echo chamber, your idea might seem original to you, but it might not actually *be* an original. Even if it's been done before, it doesn't mean that you can't do it, too. How many Italian restaurants are there? How many pizza places are there? They all do it in different ways. Competition is a good thing—it means that there is a market for your idea. Don't discount yourself because you're not some big name yet.

Mistake #11 - Not Focusing on the Importance of Building an Email List

Building an email list is very important especially when you consider that we don't own our social media platforms. In 2019, both Facebook and Instagram went down and caused a major uproar when they were inaccessible. Think of it this way: Mr. Zuckerberg is your landlord and he rents you space on Facebook. At any time, he can shut it down, kick you out, and you'll lose access to all the contacts you've built up over time. The only way you can avoid catastrophe is to curate your own contacts by building your own email list. Once you have someone's email, you get direct contact with them. Not building an email list soon enough in the promotional process is one way to delay results.

Mistake #12 - Putting All Your Eggs in the Social Media Basket

If you don't have a website and you're not collecting email addresses, you are relying on other platforms to promote yourself and get yourself out there. That is a very slippery slope because remember, Mr. Zuckerberg is your landlord. He dictates access and price, and he can make algorithm changes. He can change the agreements anytime to the way we use the platform. Even though it's free to have a social media page or account, as a business who wants to reach a targeted audience, paying for advertising will provide great results.

Mistake #13 - Confusing Amazon with a Bookstore

There are many book distributors online but the majority of the market buys books from Amazon. It has a very large reach, especially here in the USA. What we may overlook about Amazon is that it's a search engine, not a bookstore. Publishing a book and hoping that somebody will discover it is a rookie mistake. Think about when you search for something on Google or YouTube or Amazon, you type in keywords or phrases. Amazon behaves like a search engine and is organized through an algorithm. It's designed to categorize and organize its products to give the user the best possible match. When you have used keywords, categories, and a well-written book description, the algorithm recognizes that your book is valuable and shows it to more people.

Mistake #14 - Not Sharing about Your Book Project Early Enough

If you are thinking about writing a book, post on social media, show a picture of you at the coffee shop typing. The solution to getting unstuck is involving your friends, family, and community right from the start. It builds connection and community over a shared goal. If you are trying to find motivation to get over writer's block, share the process. People love being behind the scenes. It's why things like *America's Got Talent* and *American Idol* did so well as we love watching the process; it's so addictive.

Don't be afraid to ask for feedback. Accepting criticism along the way is important when you involve people early. If you have a few ideas of what you want to write about, you can ask your audience and friends to help you decide so you write the right book. Based on the feedback I received from people with my first book, I changed the title and adjusted some of the content to ensure it fit the right audience. Being willing to course correct is super important and will save you a lot of effort in the future.

Mistake #15 - Not Creating Automated Solutions that Work while You Sleep

If you're on the hamster wheel constantly creating content, you will burn out. Trying to keep up by posting online 12 times a day is not sustainable. Granted, you have to stay current by keeping your audience up-to-date. However, there are systems that you can use to automate some of the repeatable tasks so you can find the time to do other things. What I like to do with my clients is set up a funnel framework. These systems are designed to work while you sleep like sending automated emails when people join your email list. While you focus on filling the top of your funnel, creating new content and engaging with your audience, it keeps working for you consistently. That is how you get brand recognition. By consistently showing up and being associated with the kind of content you stand for. If your audience keeps seeing your name posting valuable content, you're staying front of mind.

Mistake #16 - Not Measuring Results

You need to follow steps and implement each of the steps, then measure every part of the process and tweak as you go along. Even though you might start with an idea, where you end up with may differ if you're not measuring results. You can change a strategy based on your results, whether good or bad. Is posting in a Facebook group getting new readers? Is running a paid Amazon ad selling books? How will you know what to focus on if you're trying too many things without a way of knowing what is working? If you don't have a way of measuring your results, you'll spin your wheels and waste your resources. A simple gauge of audience growth is how much your email list is growing. If your efforts are not consistently building your email database of fans and followers, all your efforts online will be hard to track.

4

Will It Sell?

If you have a concept or book idea, you can pitch it first to your audience to see what interests them. I have so many ideas for books I want to write, but I'm going to ask my audience first. What do you want to read? What are you struggling with right now that I can help you with? If I bring them into the process early on, they feel like they're part of it. You'll be surprised how they take ownership. When you come to publish your book or launch a business, they feel like they are one of your co-founders. It really helps to get sales in the door right in the beginning from your raving fans.

A great way of seeing the conversation is what people review. Just reading other reviews of books will give you a plethora of content ideas. If you have an idea for a book and you want to assess if there is a need in the market, just go and read the reviews.

If you're stuck, start with the very first step, a baby step. You can test your content before you commit to a big project. Write a short blog post, ask your audience questions. Invite them to an event. Invite them to download your freebie. You don't want to spend hours and hours in your closet creating something only to have it launch to crickets. When you start interacting with other people, you may realize that your idea might be a bad idea. Learn the lesson early so you can you do it differently or make your idea better.

I think this is one of the reasons why it can be hard to get a traditional publishing contract. They are so picky about what they want to publish. When you propose a book idea, it may not be about luck or if another author is more favored than you. It's whether or not the idea is sticky and if it will sell. A lot of the time, publishers have the benefit of experience and they know what people are responding to based on their sales data. If an author has an okay book idea but they have already built an audience and an email list, it's more likely they will be offered a contract. Compared to a really great book idea where the author is unknown, it's still too much of a gamble. Good thing you're reading this book so you can become hot property!

Before you start with your content creation, do a little market research. You can easily do this online for free. Things like [17] Survey Monkey or running a poll on Facebook will help you get feedback. People will speak in their own language. If you ask, *"What is your biggest struggle or challenge with X?"*, you'll be surprised what people say. You might think they're having a problem with X, but it actually turns out to be something like Y. This exercise is something I highly recommend *before* you write a book or create a product or launch a business. Do the research first. What is the point of creating content that takes time, money, and effort, and nobody wants it?

---

[17] Survey Monkey https://www.surveymonkey.com

5

What Publishers & Readers Want

P ublishing is a business. You can reduce the risk of your book proposal being rejected when you have a platform of people to help sell your books. Like any good business, it is in their interest to mitigate the risks. There is an idea that it requires at least 10,000 fans or followers or emails to get a traditional publisher's attention. Their interest is to sell more books and reduce the risk of wasting their time and money so they can scale their efforts. You become less of a risk when you can show a publisher that you have already built a following of fans, readers, and an eager audience.

What Publishers Want

When pitching a book proposal to a publisher, the question they will ask is "Who are you and why should I care?" If you are able to persuade or influence others, then you can consider yourself a thought leader with a platform of influence. This is especially true if you write non-fiction books where readers come to find a solution to their aching problems. Authority, visibility, trustworthiness, reach, and popularity all play into it. This can feel like you are competing in a popularity contest, which in essence, you are.

If you are interested in pursuing the traditionally published route of securing an agent who will pitch you to a publisher, then you must come prepared and show that you have a platform and are ready to do the marketing legwork.

What Readers Want

A survey of 6,000 readers hosted by bestselling author Marie Force offered some eye-opening statistics. Keep in mind that 50% were between the ages of 36-55 years old, and 95% of survey respondents were female.

- 88% of readers follow their favorite authors on Facebook.
- 69% of readers use Facebook to find information about their favorite author.
- 86% of readers prefer to buy their books from Amazon/Kindle.
- 35% of readers visit a physical bookstore only twice a year.
- 3% of readers care about the name of the publisher as a seal of approval, where 29% pay some attention and 28% pay no attention at all.
- Readers are 50% more likely to buy a self-published book from an author they already know.
- 60% of readers said that it doesn't matter buying a book from an unknown author.
- More than 32% hear about books they end up buying from Facebook, followed by 12% on Goodreads.
- 60% prefer to use Facebook to get information about their favorite authors, 53% get their info from the author's website, and 45% from the author's email newsletter.
- 56% of reader reviews posted to retail sites sway their purchasing decisions, and 51% of readers feel that reviews are still somewhat important.
- 43% say that a star rating is not that important and they will try a book with a low star rating if they like the cover/teaser/sample.
- Offering a free book makes it 20 times more likely that a reader will be introduced to a new author and buy subsequent books.
- 84% were extremely likely to buy a second book from an author if they enjoyed their free book.
- 70% of readers don't care about seeing "New York Times Bestseller" or "USA Today Bestseller" along the author's name.
- 87% subscribe to the newsletter of their favorite authors.

- 83% of readers like to hear news of new or upcoming releases from the authors they follow.
- 50% said if they really want the book they don't care what the price is, and 23% would not pay more than $4.99 for an eBook.
- 61% said that it does not influence their decision to buy an unknown author's book when they see an endorsement from a well-known author on the cover or blurb.
- 52% said professionalism of the cover design makes the most impact when influencing their purchasing decision.

The good news is that readers care about *you* the author, they want to connect with *you* personally, and they want to hear about your book projects directly from *you*. It shows that readers like to connect with their favorite authors online on places like Facebook, Goodreads, and on the author's own website. It shows that building an email list to communicate directly with your fans is very important. Remember, it's *real people* who read books, so what should be most important to you is pleasing your readers. Having a bestselling status badge doesn't persuade a reader to purchase a book from an author they may not already know, so breathe a sigh of relief; you don't need to sell millions of copies. Since readers prefer all kinds of formats to consume books, it's important to offer all formats like ebook, audiobook, paperback, and hardcover.

You can put your fears aside: you don't need a big name publisher to offer you a contract to realize your publishing dreams. Gone are the days of the big publishing houses controlling the access an author has with his/her readers. Today, the reader wants direct access and a personal connection with the author. You can dismiss the idea that self-publishing will be disadvantageous to your sales. The reader doesn't actually care who has published the book, only that it's a good quality and professionally created book they are interested in reading.

If self-publishing is the way you want to go, check out my training [18] Self

---

[18] Self Publishing Mastermind https://www.selfpublishingmastermind.com

Publishing Mastermind. For more help, download my free Checklist at [19] www.mimikacooney.com/rightbook

---

[19] Checklist Write the Right Book www.mimikacooney.com/rightbook

II

Part Two

PART TWO

6

Before You Start Writing

I t can be so frustrating pouring your heart out, bearing your soul, only to have your book tank and launch to crickets. For many authors, the problem arises when they spend all the time and effort in writing, only to discover after the launch that they had written the wrong book! Many times we get so excited about a book idea, that we just jump straight into writing before we've thought about important aspects. Not considering your audience first and who you are writing for can cause you to waste time. Who wants to spend all their time and effort writing a book, and it doesn't sell? That is the most disheartening thing that could happen to a writer. You've poured your ideas into a book, and you realize nobody wants to listen. I personally think that writing and publishing a book is at least a six-month project, so let's ensure your time is well spent. Let's look at how you can set yourself up for success by planning your goals and strategy so all your efforts will pay off.

Importance of Research

Before you start writing your book, it is important that you do research. This essential first step is really important to help you plan, publish, and promote a book that will actually sell. With one of my recent books, I started writing the layout. Then I thought I would do some extra research just to double check. In that process, I realized there was some very crucial elements to my topic that

I hadn't written about. So I added an additional chapter, as well as omitted content that was not relevant. Even before I started going into the meat of the content, I already knew what was important.

Another reason why doing research is so important is that you need to validate the idea first. In the marketing world, they do samples, tests, and get feedback before proceeding with the expense of producing their big idea. You always want to make sure that there is a market for your book: are people going to buy it and is there a need?

Google

Think about it, when you want to know something, where do you go first? You go to Google, right? If you search [20]Google Trends or [21]Google Keyword Planner you will see what the world is actually searching for, and you can compare ideas. This will pull in information, especially relating to the keywords that people use. Sometimes, you might think a topic is popular only to discover that it is not. Or maybe there is something that you might have missed, or you discover an untapped market.

Amazon

Amazon is primarily a search engine, not a bookstore. Searching through the different categories and seeing what the best sellers are is helpful. Discovering what is selling will help you to position your book in the right market. If you have an idea, you can tweak it to suit your particular market. For example, after doing research I realized that cowboy billionaires is a really hot romance category right now! I was like, wow, that's actually a thing?

---

[20] Google Trends https://trends.google.com/

[21] Google Keyword Planner http://bit.ly/2T1rRDi

Facebook

One of my personal favorites is doing an online poll on my Facebook page, and asking my email subscribers about an idea. I will ask what they think about a topic, what things they are struggling with, or what their biggest challenges are. This works really well for non-fiction books especially if you're writing to a felt need. You want to help people find a solution to their problem or solve their pain. For fiction writers, you want to be able to understand what concepts people are interested in.

Another reason I love to do research before I start writing is asking the audience to vote for their favorite cover option. When I do a photo shoot or have an idea for different layouts, I might think my pick is a great idea. By asking my audience, they can vote on their favorites. This does three things for me. It validates an idea I have, and it helps me save a lot of time and something that would not work. What it also does it that is primes my readers to feel invested in the project even before I hit publish. They feel like they're part of your project, so when it's published, they are more likely the people who are going to support you and buy the book.

Publisher Rocket

One of my favorite tools on the market is a software called [22]Publisher Rocket by [23]Kindlepreneur, Dave Chesson. Using this software has saved me a ton of time, and helped me narrow down keywords and categories to focus on. I usually spend a week doing forensic research on a book idea before I start writing it, and using this software helps tremendously.

---

[22] Publisher Rocket Software http://bit.ly/MimikaROCKET

[23] Kindlepreneur http://bit.ly/35zHcxk

KD Spy

This is another one of my favorite software tools that helps me identify a green light category. What this means is that [24]KD Spy does the work to crunch the numbers and will show you a list of the number of sales in a particular category. It lists the popularity, potential for profit, and competitors all neatly presented so you can see who you are up against. This way you will know how many sales you will need to achieve to attain that bestseller status, as well as identify the perfect categories and market fit.

---

[24] KD Spy Software http://bit.ly/MimikaKDSPY

7

Pick the Right Genre

Whether you are a fiction or non-fiction writer, there are certain aspects that you need to consider when selecting your genre. You can find genres within genres that will better suit your book. Say for example, you are writing a children's book, and it's about animal life on a farm, there are different age ranges that are within that genre. A chapter book is suited for kids aged 7 to 12 who are independent readers. Your book needs to be written with those genre-specific considerations like word count, number of illustrations, number of pages, style of the cover, etc.

Another consideration regarding your genre is to follow the tropes. In other words, what are those overarching ideas? Such as with romance novels: girl meets boy, boy loses girl, forbidden romance, etc.

What is the word count format? Many fiction novels typically range in the 70,000 to 100,000 word count. Non-fiction books could be anything from 15,000 and upwards. Depending on the topic, issues like word count are pertinent to its specific genre and category.

How do people like to read their books? If we think about the romance novelist, a lot of romance readers are keen readers. They read very fast and they prefer to buy eBooks so they can read it on a Kindle or a device. For non-fiction writers, if you're writing a marketing book with a lot of tips and tools, perhaps your readers prefer paperbacks so they can make notes on the side of the book. When you're thinking about your reader, you are putting yourself in their shoes and thinking about their habits, how they like to read, and what format they like to read. This will really help to narrow down what kind of book you should be writing.

8

Pick the Right Categories

No matter whether you are self-publishing or are traditionally published, conducting research into which categories to list your book is vitally important. Perhaps you're writing a business book about marketing. The marketing genre is very broad. If you publish your book in that one category, it's going to get lost in a sea of millions of other marketing books. If the category your book is listed in has 100,000 books, then your book is going to get lost. But if your book is in a sub-category of maybe 100 books, your book becomes more visible to potential readers since competition is less.

In the research process, you're going to start digging a little deeper to uncover the sub-categories. These will help you niche down into a particular area so your book is more easily found. With Amazon, you can list your book within two browse categories, and include up to 7 keywords. These browse categories are often very broad, and not always relevant. When you set up your book in your Amazon KDP account, you can select the categories that you think are the best. Once you have your book uploaded and it's visible in the Amazon store, you can [25]email Amazon and ask them to add your book to up to 10 other categories. If you are within a less competitive category, the likelihood of you achieving bestseller status is more probable.

---

[25] Email Amazon USA https://kdp.amazon.com/en_US/contact

How Amazon works is that it looks at the category and which is the top selling book within the category based on the number of sales. The price of the book does not affect the rating, only the number of downloads for that particular category, for that particular day or hour. The price could be 99 cents or $9.99 as it really depends on how many units are downloaded. For example, if you are selling your book for 99 cents and you sell a thousand copies, you're going to bump to the top of the list (but might not earn the most money).

By picking a smaller category, you have less competition and you increase your chances of reaching that bestseller status. Once you achieve the orange "Best Seller" badge, Amazon and its cleverness decide that your book must be valuable and starts showing it in other relevant categories. That way, you can start rising up into those broader categories as your downloads increase. This is why I feel it's so important that you know what this plan is, what you're aiming for, and narrow down exactly what you need to achieve.

To help you narrow down the best categories, use [26]Publisher Rocket and [27] KD Spy and read this helpful article on [28]how to choose categories.

---

[26] Publisher Rocket Software http://bit.ly/MimikaROCKET

[27] KD Spy Software http://bit.ly/MimikaKDSPY

[28] How to Choose Categories article http://bit.ly/2Nja0Ef

9

Pick the Right Keywords

One mistake first time authors make is selecting a random list of keywords by simply guessing. When you upload your book to Amazon and your KDP dashboard, you can list up to 7 keywords. Instead of single word keywords, rather use phrases of two to three words for more relevancy. Keyword phrases work better than single words. This is where your research proves very useful. For example, if your book is related to confidence and faith, using the keywords "faith" or "confidence" might seem logical, but are too broad. By doing your research, you can match the right keywords to what people are searching for. Instead you can use "Build confidence and self-esteem" or "Christian living for women". Using the correct keywords within your book description will also help you rank higher in the category list. A good category and keyword selection are going to be important when you run Amazon ads.

Amazon is constantly searching using its algorithm by trawling through book descriptions. It's looking for keywords and categories, and matching them to search results. Keyword phrases are going to be important as you will use them within your book description and blurb. What you put on the back cover and how you describe your book are going to help your book to be discovered.

The tool I love to use is called [29]KD Spy. This is software that you buy upfront, and that you download to your computer and it is accessible through your navigation bar. What I love about it is that it works hand in hand with [30]Publisher Rocket software. Publisher Rocket gives you categories and keywords, with KD Spy you can see the sales and competition in greater detail. If your book is listed within a category, say children's books about farm life, you can click on the button and a pop-up opens. It will show you the top 100 bestselling books in that category with their sales values, links to their sales page, and other links. By knowing how the competing books are performing, you are better able to plan and set goals.

You can do research manually by going through Amazon and using a spreadsheet to find the categories and keywords that other books are using. It's not always obvious, and it is very time-consuming, but it can be done (especially if you don't want to buy the software).

[29] KD Spy Software http://bit.ly/MimikaKDSPY

[30] Publisher Rocket Software http://bit.ly/MimikaROCKET

III

Part Three

10

Writing Stage

N ow that you know whom you are writing for and the right genre and categories, you can plan the outline and book layout. Having done your research will help speed up the writing stage because you won't have to waste time guessing what to write about.

What Kind of a Writer are You?

We are all at different stages of our writing and development, and we all have different goals. Once you understand where you are, you can work toward where you want to be. I have a quiz on my website [31] "What Kind of Writer are You?" that you can take for free to determine what stage you are at and strategies to help you. It's exciting no matter where you are in your writing journey, because it means you have room for improvement and you can always get to the next level. So let's look at these a little closer at each stage.

Hobby Writer

At this stage, you haven't started writing your book yet; it's just an idea. You don't have an email list, or you don't know much about marketing. Perhaps

---

[31] What Kind of Writer are You Free Quiz http://mimikacooney.com/quiz

you're struggling to get started. Maybe you like to write for enjoyment and just as a hobby. Maybe writing is cathartic and a way of processing past pain and experiences. There is no real pressure to publish as it doesn't matter if anyone reads what you write. You don't really know who you are writing your book for, or who your audience is. You haven't started putting your writing online or tried any marketing, it's just between you and the keyboard. Your writing is good, but you're not sure what to do next. Perhaps you have difficulty figuring out your messaging or what the felt need is. Perhaps you struggle with writer's block as every time you sit down to write, you feel stuck. Maybe marketing is not your jam and you have no clue where to start or what to do next. You're not sure if you should self-publish or if pursuing an agent is worth it.

Casual Writer

At this stage, you need help getting clear on who your audience is, and you don't know exactly who you're writing for. Perhaps you have ambitions of becoming a full-time author so you can make money from your books. You may be seeking a publishing contract or an agent, and you've looked into the publishing paths. Perhaps you have an email list but you don't necessarily send out regular emails. Maybe you don't know much about marketing or what you should do to attract readers to build your fans and your email subscribers.

Maybe you haven't figured out how to build your author platform, what your signature brand is, or how to attract those ideal readers. Perhaps you're busy writing your book and/or editing it, and you feel a little stuck with what to do next.

Serious Writer

You have ambitions of becoming a full-time author and you want to use a book to build your business/ministry, attract leads, boost your visibility and elevate your authority. You know who your audience is, and who you're writing your book for, but may need help finding your ideal readers. You're interested in self-publishing as a means to get your book to market fast, and you want to keep control of the profits and the process. Perhaps your book is ready for print and you are in the final editing stage.

You need help with marketing and publishing. You regularly communicate and send emails to your tribe, so you've already started building a fan base. You may be having trouble getting your marketing to work, as you've tried things and wasted a lot of money on things that didn't work. You've thrown a bunch of spaghetti at the wall hoping it would stick, and you need clarity of what to do next. Maybe you're interested in securing a publisher and an agent to pursue the traditional publishing route. You're thinking about what self-publishing could mean for you. You feel time-strapped and you need help scaling your efforts because you're busy writing and managing your business/ministry. Perhaps you're getting invited to speak on podcasts or at churches, and you need help setting up your marketing funnel. You want to reach more people and create systems that work on autopilot. You need help with growing your author platform, building your email list, setting up Facebook ads, and applying best marketing practices to grow your writing career into a business. You're ready to invest in yourself and your writing career to scale to the next step.

Knowledge Is Key

When you have a burning desire to write and share your message, the overwhelm can take over. It can feel like you're drinking from a fire hose! By understanding why you want to write, and who you are writing for, will really help. When you have your big "why" in front of you, you can progress to figuring out whom you're writing for. This is important because if you have that big why firmly established, when it gets tough (and believe me, writing a book can be hard work), you'll stick with it. Once the romance and excitement of writing a book wear off, that is when the real work begins. Having the fortitude to get through the "messy middle" is what separates the real writers from the wannabes.

A big mistake I see authors make in writing and publishing books is that they feel like their book can speak to everyone, yet it connects with no one. If you don't have that ideal avatar reader in mind, your writing just becomes a jumbled mass of thoughts on paper and perhaps just a diary. That is not to say writing your thoughts and ideas like a diary is bad. Many writers write purely for the enjoyment and as a legacy. But if you are thinking of your book as a tool to reach people, to help and serve people, you need a different mindset.

When you think of your book from the reader's perspective, you write differently. Reading is a very personal experience. That reader is not sitting in a crowded room listening to you speak. They are reading your book on their own, in perhaps a private setting. You are having a one-on-one conversation with that person. If you think of that person sitting on the other side of the table from you, like you're enjoying a cup of coffee together, what would you say? What state of mind are they in? You are then able to collect your thoughts and share your message in a way that connects with that reader. You are creating a book that is going to speak to them personally, and solve that problem or satisfy that need.

No matter which kind of writer you are, you're on the right path. Following a process is going to help you take your writing from where you are now, and growing it to the next level so you can achieve your goals. If you would like more tools to help you move to the next level, check out my [32]resources and my course [33]Self Publishing Mastermind.

---

[32] Resources https://www.mimikacooney.com/resources

[33] Self Publishing Mastermind https://www.selfpublishingmastermind.com

11

Writing Style

When it comes to the craft of writing, there is no one size fits all. Your life experiences, knowledge, expertise, and worldview will shape how you write, why you write, and who you write for. Personally, I find speaking my thoughts out loud easier than sitting down to write (especially for non-fiction content). I need to speak it out first to get the thoughts out of my mind. What I do to break writer's block is to speak to my phone and have it transcribed. With my more creative content (like fiction writing), I will start with a prompt and let my thoughts flow as I type. So it really just depends on what works for you.

Figuring out your own creative writing flow takes a little experimentation and practice. In the writing world, we refer to two styles of writers, but I like to add a third.

Planner

The first kind of writing style is called the Planner. These writers are the ones that like the methodology of creating an outline, with a specific plan and layout for their book decided in advance. This style works for you if you prefer to write a thorough book proposal and outline with a step-by-step approach to what each chapter is going to cover. A book proposal is a must if you plan to pitch your book idea to agents and publishers. With non-fiction books, you write the proposal *before* you start writing; whereas fiction writers need to have the book completed first before seeking representation. The exercise of creating an outline is very useful knowing exactly who your market is, and how you plan to write your book. The traditional publishing model has expected this format from writers for years, but it doesn't always work for *every* writer. If you like to let your creativity flow, this style can frustrate you since you've committed to sticking with a plan. Oftentimes, writers give up and don't finish their book because this writing style feels restricted with the planner approach.

Panster

On the flip side, there is the kind of writing style called the Panster. Ever heard of the saying "flying by the seat of your pants"? A Panster doesn't start with a plan, or have an outline. They go "with the flow" of where their writing spontaneously takes them. This style works well if you prefer not to have constraints and want to keep an open mind of where your book will end up. Stephen King is known for this style, of writing his characters in and out of difficult situations he finds them in. Of course, he's written so many books that he knows what works for him. But for some writers, this style can feel uncomfortable and too loosey-goosey. The movies have romanticized the writer sitting at the typewriter and this perfect prose just flows forth. Often this is not reality; there is still a lot of work to be done.

Playwright

The third writing style I like to refer to I call the Playwright. Personally, this style works best for me. It combines a little bit of the Planner and a little bit of the Panster. As a playwright, the audience and the characters are very important to the story, as well as the plot. If you think of a play, you have the beginning, the middle, and the end. The audience is taken on a journey. Where are you taking the reader? No matter whether it's fiction or non-fiction, thinking of the reader (or audience) and how they will experience the reading journey helps to put the pieces into place. For non-fiction, describing who your reader is and the problem they have helps you to focus on the outcome or result they are looking for. For fiction, having the reader fall in love with the characters and following a story arc will hook them. Who is the protagonist in the story? What is life like for that person? What do they have to achieve or overcome? We can start to plot and plan where the book is going based on the reader experience. The goal of any book is to take the reader from point A to point Z on a journey. Laying out the story arc and reader journey helps to solidify the writing plan. Joseph Campbell coined the term [34] "The Hero's Journey" which most Hollywood movies follow. When you are thinking of the reader, you are thinking of the content and how it fits in with their expectations. You can better plan the overall outline and structure, but leave room for creative flow within each chapter.

You don't need to feel like you have to do one or the other. The only way you'll know what works for you is to try each method. It has to fit your particular style, your personality, and the time that you have available to write. Once you know what works for you, it will really help make the book writing process a lot smoother.

---

[34] The Hero's Journey https://en.wikipedia.org/wiki/Hero's_journey

12

How to Get Your Book Done

There are a few ways to get your book done. You can either write it from scratch using a detailed outline, or you can piece together bits of content into a logical flow. Every book I've written never turned out exactly how I originally planned it at the start. I've written several books, blog posts, and content where I have just the titles to start with. I know what I'm going to write about, and I start writing, and go back and edit later. My favorite way to break through that writer's block of staring at a blank screen is to speak it. If I have something that I can talk about quicker than I can write, I will do audio to text. Whether it's teaching a webinar or a podcast, recording it on an app and then transcribing it, I use whatever works. The point is to get the ideas out of your head and onto paper as the editing can be done later. You can't edit what you don't write, so get busy writing!

Another way to get a book done fast, especially if you're super busy and have the money, is to hire a ghostwriter. This is a professional writer whose job is to piece together the information and write it in your voice, and you take the credit. Usually a ghostwriter will interview you to get the story and idea of what you like to say. Then they will write the book for you. This is a popular option in the business world where a subject matter expert has the knowledge, but not necessarily the time to sit down and write. It is, of course, more expensive as you are hiring out every stage of the process, but is a good investment if the book becomes a lead generator for a business.

Another alternative is to work with a writing coach or an editor. They will work with you step-by-step and guide you along the writing process. Often, traditional publishers provide a writing coach or editor for authors to work with so they meet the contract obligations and the set deadline. It helps to keep the writer accountable.

All of these methods can work; you just need to find the flow that works for you.

Goal Setting

The reason why goal setting is important is that the idea of writing a book sounds great, but it's the completion and execution that really matters. According to writer [35]Joseph Epstein who wrote an article in the New York Times, "81 percent of Americans feel that they have a book in them". That's approximately 200 million people who aspire to become authors. Another statistic shows that 97% of writers never finish their book!

Epstein goes on to say in his *New York Times* article, "Before I had first done so, writing a book seemed a fine, even grand thing. And so it still seems — except, truth to tell, it is a lot better to have written a book than to actually be writing one. Without attempting to overdo the drama of the difficulty of writing, to be in the middle of composing a book is almost always to feel oneself in a state of confusion, doubt and mental imprisonment, with an accompanying intense wish that one worked instead at bricklaying."

Writing a book takes discipline, a plan, and the fortitude to finish. Having an outline is really helpful to keep you on task and on point so you don't go off on a tangent. Personally, I use a spreadsheet to help me track my daily word count and progress. When you start, writing a hundred words may feel daunting, but tracking your daily effort keeps you moving forward. Your word count will increase as you flex your writing muscle. Every little bit counts so don't get discouraged if you feel some days you write less or more than your plan.

---

[35] Joseph Epstein article https://nyti.ms/2FrhfFD

Another good thing to have is a publication deadline to force you to take action. Instead of lamenting over your book for years, and the idea keeps you up at night, set a date. You can dream about it for years, but unless you set a deadline, nothing gets done. It adds pressure, but it will force you to take action. Finding an accountability partner is huge. If you're working with the publisher, they will keep you accountable and make sure that you do what's needed to meet the deadline. At the end of the day, you need to get that first draft done. A lot of authors get stuck thinking it has to be perfect. Never edit while writing; just get your first draft done. If it's in your head, nobody can read it, right? Even if it sounds like a hot mess, you don't want to edit while you write as it will slow the whole process down. If you can just get it down on paper, you can edit what you write. I always say the first draft is you split spitting out all the ideas that you have, and it might not make sense. Once you have your first draft, you can put your editing hat on and go back to make it sound fancy.

Many writers never finish their books because they get so fixated on it being perfect; and done is better than perfect! Getting it done and tweaking along the way, and having a second set of eyes will help you get your book done.

IV

Part Four

13

Importance of Editing

Y ou know that thing you do when you've looked at something so many times that you stop seeing it? Like a wall hanging you've walked past a hundred times, but don't actually "see" it. This is why editing is super important. Save your budget for someone who is a professional, not your auntie or your sister or your friend. They mean well, but you need an objective set of eyes to look over your work. To have a professional product, you need to treat your book professionally. It's important to find an unbiased editor and/or proofreader to help you fix any grammatical, spelling, or sentence structure issues. No matter how many times you read through your manuscript, there are bound to be errors you miss. An editor can do either line editing, or basic proofreading. You want somebody who doesn't know you, who can look for those mistakes. Believe me, if you skip on editing, you will get crucified with bad reviews! Bad reviews will affect your future sales and make it harder to convince readers of the quality of your writing.

Inviting early beta readers to help read through your book will pick up mistakes. They may not be professional editors but they are enthusiastic. I personally like to build a book launch team for each book launch. I have a group of wonderful supporters whom I give early access, before the rest of the world gets to read my book. They are going to read it before it goes to publication and often they will pick up mistakes that even the editor might have missed.

And another tool you can use is to read your book aloud. You can complete two tasks in one by recording an audio book, and simultaneously pick out any mistakes. When you read aloud you use a different part of your brain, so you take yourself out of editing and are more objective. If you find content that doesn't work, you can go back and edit your book while you are doing your audio book, and speed up your workflow.

Another investment you don't want to skimp on is a professionally designed cover. The saying is true, we do judge a book by its cover whether we like it or not. If a potential reader is not enticed by your cover, how are they going to know about your fabulous writing? Make the investment and have a professional provide you with options. Some of my favorite tools are [36] 99Designs ; [37] Reedsy and Fiverr for finding designers and contractors.

---

[36] 99 Designs http://bit.ly/37LKFu2

[37] Reedsy http://bit.ly/2T2kjzW

14

Publishing Your Book

So you have done your research, you know what categories, genre and keywords you are going to be using. You know who you are writing your book for, and know the felt need of your ideal reader. The next stage is getting your book to market by publishing it. There are several ways and means about doing this.

Pick Your Path

The first task is to pick your publishing path. Perhaps you want to pursue a traditional publishing path, and this is great if you can secure a contract. You may get paid upfront, but it depends on how big of an author platform or the reach you have. This is why building your author platform first is super important. Refer to my book [38]Build Your Author Platform with a Purpose: Marketing Strategies for Writers for more help on platform building.

Traditional Publishing

---

[38] Build Your Author Platform with a Purpose: Marketing Strategies for Writers https://www. mimikacooney.com/platformlinks

Pros

One of the pros about traditional publishing is that the publisher has a wide distribution network. It's much easier to get into bookstores with traditional publishers because they have that established relationship, as many bookstores and libraries will not order directly from Amazon. They prefer to purchase from the publisher directly because they get a wholesale discount. Many aspiring writers think, if you want to get into bookstores or libraries, you have to be traditionally published. This is not necessarily true for indie authors. The publishing industry has changed significantly over the past few years with the introduction of digital books and online sales avenues. Many more people are buying books online from distributors like Amazon, so the old school publishers don't have the same clout they used to have. Another pro for traditional publishing is that they will cover all the production costs to get the book to market. This includes editing, cover design, formatting, and distribution.

Cons

The downside to traditional publishing is that it is very slow to market. It is very time-consuming writing a book proposal and pitching publishers (which often results in rejection). Simply getting someone to believe in your book idea can take months or even years! Once you secure a book contract, the publisher may give the writer 9 to 12 months to finish writing the book (especially with non-fiction). By the time they edit, format and complete the layout, you're looking at a good one to two years before you see that book hit the market. It is also very competitive to pitch your book to publishers because they are very picky and have limited resources. The market is flooded with aspiring authors and they might not risk their money on an unknown author. They want to know that their investment is going to yield a return.

The other downside of traditional publishing is that authors don't make much money. Typically, traditionally published authors earns 10% commission from book sales. After the publisher takes off their costs and their commission, you're very lucky if you can get 3% profit. To make a decent living you need to sell thousands of books. With books I have traditionally published in the past, I receive a check every six months for the previous six month of sales. It's certainly not anything to write home about because I'm left with very little, usually just enough to pay for one lunch!

Another downside of traditional publishing is that they do very minimal marketing. Some smaller, more progressive publishers might be more invested in the marketing process. The average is that bigger publishers still expect the author to do the bulk of the work. Many aspiring writers believe that if you get a book contract, that writing the book is all that is required. However, publishers are now expecting authors to do even more marketing than they did in the past. They are doing less and less because they have limited resources. They are only going to invest their time and money into an author in whom they can get a return on their investment. The truth is that it is still up to you as the writer to do your own marketing. You still have to put yourself out there, you still have to build your email list, and you still have to put in the effort to promote your book.

Another very important aspect that many aspiring writers overlook is the rights. When you sign a contract with a traditional publisher, often you are handing over all the rights to your book. In other words, they can reuse your book without your permission to create different formats, translations, and perhaps anthologies. Of course, it is a good thing to create more products and revenue streams from your book, but not every publisher agrees to compensate the author for these additions. If you ever want to do something else with your book, like create an audio book, change the cover or keywords or categories, or sell the rights to make a movie, you may be limited. You will have a problem because the traditional publisher now owns the rights. You will have to get their permission to do anything with *your* book! I've heard many stories of authors buying back their rights because they could not do anything more with their book and wanted control.

Self-Publishing

Pros

With self-publishing you have complete control. You get to pick the style, title, cover and layout. It's very quick to market. You can literally have an idea for a book, write it on the weekend, and have it published in a few days. However, I don't advise this because you definitely do not want to put out junk. Unfortunately, self-publishing has got a bad rap from inexperienced writers who don't take the time to produce a good quality product.

Personally, I like to get an idea for a book and put out feelers in the market to assess if there is a need. If it's hot right now and people are searching for the topic, they want to know about it now. Who cares what happens in two years? That book needs to be published now! The nice thing about self-publishing is that you can have a very short turnaround. You decide when the publication date is, and you can plan accordingly.

You earn 35-70% commission when you upload your book. You are going to see the profits sooner and the money will be in your bank account within 60-90 days after the initial sale. You can monitor exactly the sales you make, and you have the control of your genre, categories, and keywords. If something isn't working, you have the access and control to test and try things to improve your books performance.

Cons

The big con of self-publishing is that you have to cover all the production costs yourself. You pay for the cover design, editing, layout, and formatting. However, the good news is that with a small budget you can get it all done. You need to take a long-term view. Even though it will take some time to earn the money back, in the long-term, it is more beneficial. Your book is an asset and any investment you make, you will see the rewards for years to come long after you hit publish.

Sometimes, it's harder to get into libraries and bookstores if you don't have an established relationship. If you can't get your book on display at your local brick-and-mortar store, it is not a major negative because most people don't buy their books from bookstores anymore. Most people buy their books online where there is a much larger distribution and potential for sales. Many bestselling books you see on Amazon today are actually self-published, and you probably couldn't tell the difference.

Having pursued the path of traditional publishing and experienced frustration due to limited control, I'm a big fan of self-publishing. I am now able to produce a lot more books a lot faster, and I'm able to grow my income a lot quicker, because I have the control to make changes quickly. If you spend the time, effort, and money into creating a really good product, and market it right, it will sell.

15

Build a Launch Team

B efore you start writing a book, think of building a launch or support team. Bringing people along for the journey who love and support you will prove extremely valuable when you publish your book. You want the support of a network of supporters who can give you critical feedback. You are writing to the market that has an interest in what you have to write about to bring them along for the ride. You can learn more about building your Author Platform of supporters and fans in my book [39] Build Your Author Platform with a Purpose: Marketing Strategies for Writers.

Books do not sell themselves. Publishing a book is not simply uploading it to Amazon, thinking you're done; that is not how it works. You have to put the effort into promoting your book. Letting people know about it and getting the enthusiasm and excitement built up before publish day is vital. This is especially important if you want to grab a spot on the bestseller list. When your book hits the market, you can achieve the bestseller list in your preferred category because Amazon and the other distributors look at the number of sales for that day. The bestseller list is based on the number of downloads, not on the amount of money a book is making, so the price is irrelevant.

You can ask for feedback and ideas along the way. Even while you're writing,

---

[39] Build Your Author Platform with a Purpose: Marketing Strategies for Writers https://www. mimikacooney.com/platformlinks

you can involve your audience. In my Facebook group, I will ask for feedback on anything from a book concept idea, the title, description and cover design.

Getting feedback is invaluable and having the help to promote and sell the book through reviews and sharing is super important. Once a book is live, it's crucial to get reviews uploaded as soon as possible. This is when you encourage your fans and book launch team to add their reviews as soon as possible so the Amazon algorithm picks up that your book is popular. Reviews will help with future sales and will help you rank your book higher.

When you're ready to do it again, all you need to do is to rinse and repeat. The system will work for any book you want to write. This is the same process I use for every book before I even write it. I might think it's a great idea, but if a market isn't going to buy, I am not going to waste my time.

Hopefully this book has been useful to you to help you reduce the overwhelm, get more structured in the way you approach your book writing, and help you to write that book fast. When you have a system in place, you know whom you're writing for, and have set your goals, then you're on your way to success. Get ready to enjoy the success of being a bestselling author!

Come and join my private Facebook Group [40]Mimika Insiders and connect with other like-minded Christian writers, entrepreneurs and ministers. To learn more about me and my resources visit [41]www.mimikacooney.com

---

[40] Mimika Insider Group https://www.mimikacooney.com/insiders

[41] Mimika Cooney website https://www.mimikacooney.com/

16

Favorite Tools

H ere are some of my favorite tools that I personally use for writing my books:

KD Spy Software

One of my go-to tools I use before I start writing is to use [42] KD Spy to research categories, genres, competitors and keywords. I'm quickly able to assess where I should position my book, and what the important categories to focus on.

Scrivener

With [43] Scrivener software you buy and download it to your computer. It is great for writing and formatting, and getting it into the right format (especially for printed books). It does have a higher learning curve because there are a lot of things that the software does, and it can be a little overwhelming. Once you get used to it, you can do things like add tags, references, annotations and export the formatted book.

---

[42] KD Spy Software http://bit.ly/MimikaKDSPY

[43] Scrivener http://bit.ly/2NjaDh5

Reedsy

[44]Reedsy helps writers write and organize the book structure, layout and formatting. You can easily move chapters with their drag and drop feature for simplified editing. They have a marketplace where you can find a contractor to help with editing, proofreading, design, etc.

Fiverr

With [45]Fiverr you can find a contractor for graphics, cover design, editing, or social media. You can find project listed starting at $5, and you can create your own projects contracts can bid on at a very reasonable rate.

99Designs

With [46]99Designs you can create a contest and have multiple professional designers provide their ideas for your cover artwork. You can have 10 to 30 different designers come up with different ideas for your book cover so you have a variety to choose from. If you have a really badly designed cover with old fashioned fonts, it's just going to scream amateur and it will affect your sales. The investment made into a professional design will pay dividends.

Ingram Spark

[47]Ingram Spark is a smaller division of Ingram which is a huge book publisher. They have been around for years and they have a massive distribution network. With Ingram Spark, you can upload and print paperbacks and hardcover in a variety of sizes and paper styles. They also offer ebook distribution.

---

44 Reedsy http://bit.ly/2T2kjzW

45 Fiverr http://bit.ly/2T0gFGN

46 99 Designs http://bit.ly/37LKFu2

47 Ingram Spark https://ingramspark.com

Draft 2 Digital

[48]Draft2Digital saves you time uploading your book to the online distributors like Google books, Apple iBooks, Kobo, and all the online retailers. There is no upfront cost as they will take a small commission from the book sales.

KD Roi

[49]KD Roi is a software that helps you submit your Kindle book promotion to over 32 sites in 15 seconds without leaving Amazon, filling in mindless forms, or outsourcing to Fiverr. Run free or discounted promotions to drive traffic to your book sales page.

Active Campaign

A CRM [50]Active Campaign software helps you manage, organize and send email newsletter campaigns. With advanced features like tags you can easily automate your book funnel to work while you sleep.

Thinkific

Turn your knowledge into a profit online course using [51]Thinkific and earn additional review from your books.

---

[48] Draft 2 Digital http://bit.ly/2s6tJQ2

[49] KD Roi Software http://bit.ly/2QxfWvi

[50] Active Campaign Email Software http://bit.ly/2ZYkCxa

[51] Thinkific Course Platform http://bit.ly/39O6mf9

Author Cats Website Design

[52] Author Cats saves you the hassle and headache of creating an author website by using this turn key solution. With ready made templates designed exclusively for authors, you can have a high converting author website in no time.

Creative Market

[53]Creative Market offers ready-made graphics, templates and tools to make your visual branding pop. If you're looking for a book cover design, custom fonts, or templates; you'll find them here at affordable prices.

Canva

One of my favorite tools [54]Canva makes designing graphics so easy using their templates and royalty free stock photos.

---

[52] Author Cats Website Design http://bit.ly/304wL3J

[53] Creative Market http://bit.ly/2N1IPxe

[54] Canva http://bit.ly/2FwCi9C

Disclaimer: Please note that some of the links mentioned are affiliate links and I will earn a commission if you purchase through these links. As an Amazon Associate I earn advertising fees from qualifying purchases. I recommend these products and services as they are companies that I have found to be helpful and trustworthy. However, I do not take responsibility for any inaccuracies, loss or damage resulting from any recommendation.

About the Author

Mimika Cooney is a Bestselling Author, host of "Mimika TV" Podcast, Entrepreneur, and Award-Winning Photographer. Huffington Post nominated Mimika as one of "50 Women Entrepreneurs to Follow in 2017".

Mimika has published books in the Business/Marketing, and Christian Living genres. Her book "Mindset Make-Over: How to Renew your Mind and Walk in God's Authority" remained in the top 5 positions on Amazon for 12 months since publication. The book "Worrier to Warrior: A Mother's Journey from Fear to Faith" launched as an Amazon #1 Bestseller.

She is the creator of courses that help aspiring writers, speakers, ministers and entrepreneurs with their marketing and book publishing.

Mimika is passionate about empowering and equipping individuals to fulfill their God-given purpose, position their value, spread their message and make an impact in the marketplace. Mimika loves to spark honest conversations, blaze a trail where others fear to tread, and infuse positivity wherever she goes. She is known for building community, creating connections and helping others share their story with passion and purpose.

Mimika is a native of South Africa and citizen of the USA. She is a ferocious reader, enjoys watching soppy rom coms and cuddling on the sofa with her 3 kids and dashing husband of 24 years. When she is not dreaming up creative concepts, writing books or hosting her podcast; she will be found perfecting her spins on the ice as a competitive adult figure skater.

You can connect with me on:

🌐 https://www.mimikacooney.com

🐦 https://www.twitter.com/mimikacooney

📘 https://www.facebook.com/TheMimikaCooney

🔗 https://www.selfpublishingmastermind.com

🔗 https://www.instagram.com/MimikaCooney

🔗 https://youtube.com/c/mimikacooney

🔗 https://www.pinterest.com/mimikacooney

Subscribe to my newsletter:

✉ https://www.mimikacooney.com/rightbook

Also by Mimika Cooney

Build Your Author Platform with a Purpose: Marketing Strategies for Writers

https://www.shopmimika.com/collections/video-training/products/build-your-platform-with-a-purpose-author-signed-paperback

Building an Author Platform from the ground up as a writer can seem daunting, especially if marketing is not your jam. Authors are now expected to do more and more work to promote their own books as publishers are not interested in invisible authors. It's imperative that writers take control of their marketing, and build their author platform online.

This book will take you through an accelerated author brand development process. The strategies shared will walk you through the process to create a powerful personal brand. You will discover how designing a personal brand and identity is tied to your strengths and your unique writing style.

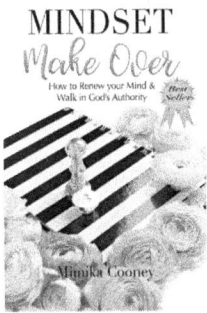

Mindset Make Over: How to Renew Your Mind and Walk in God's Authority

https://www.shopmimika.com/collections/video-training/products/mindset-make-over-video-training

AMAZON BESTSELLING BOOK for 12 Months

Do you feel worried, afraid, anxious, doubtful, angry, depressed, confused? Do you know God is calling you to greatness but you feel far from great? Are your relationships a hot mess and the daily drama drains you? Do you feel out of control but you crave peace? Are you sick and tired of being sick and tired? Are you stuck thinking of the worst case scenario for everything?

Do you feel far from God yet you crave intimacy?

If you are ready to ditch the excuses and take back your authority as a child of God then this book is for you!

With several quotes and short stories about overcoming fear, this Christian book for women will offer inspiration to overcome anxiety with confidence.

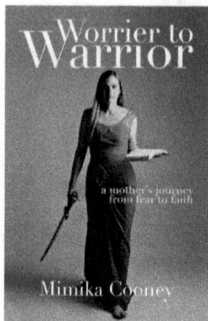

Worrier to Warrior: A Mother's Journey from Fear to Faith

https://www.shopmimika.com/collections/video-training/products/worrier-to-warrior-a-mothers-journey-from-fear-to-faith-author-signed-print-book

This is a powerful spiritual warfare manual for women seeking empowerment. The insights shared in this book will give you a battle plan you need to create a life outside of worry, so you can become the undefeated royal warrior princess that you are! You're in the middle of spiritual warfare with an unseen enemy. He is wreaking havoc in your home, family and life. As a Christian women living in a modern world, you need effective tools to fight your battles and win!

"Worrier to Warrior" is a true story of one mother's harsh reality struggling through grief, depression, suicide, burnout, failure, anxiety and lost hope.

Mimika shares her own personal and emotional journey of navigating through the fears, the shame, and the struggle surrounded by this reality. This story will open your heart and mind to things you have become numb to, because your spiritual eyes and ears have been dulled by the shame based mentality of the world. "Worrier to Warrior" is an inspirational book about hope, through the eternal love God has for each of us! Break free from the mental prison that keeps you in dark places and thrive in the light of God's Word so you can become the warrior you are meant to be!

www.ingramcontent.com/pod-product-compliance
Lightning Source LLC
Chambersburg PA
CBHW071140280326
41935CB00010B/1308